I0494300

Japanese Girls

Hot Sexy Japanese Lingerie Girls Models Pictures

By **PHOTO ART LOVER**

Copyright © Japanese Girls

All rights reserved. No part of this document may be
Reproduced or transmitted in any form or by any means, electronic, mechanical, photocopying,
Recording, or otherwise, without prior written permission of photo art lover.

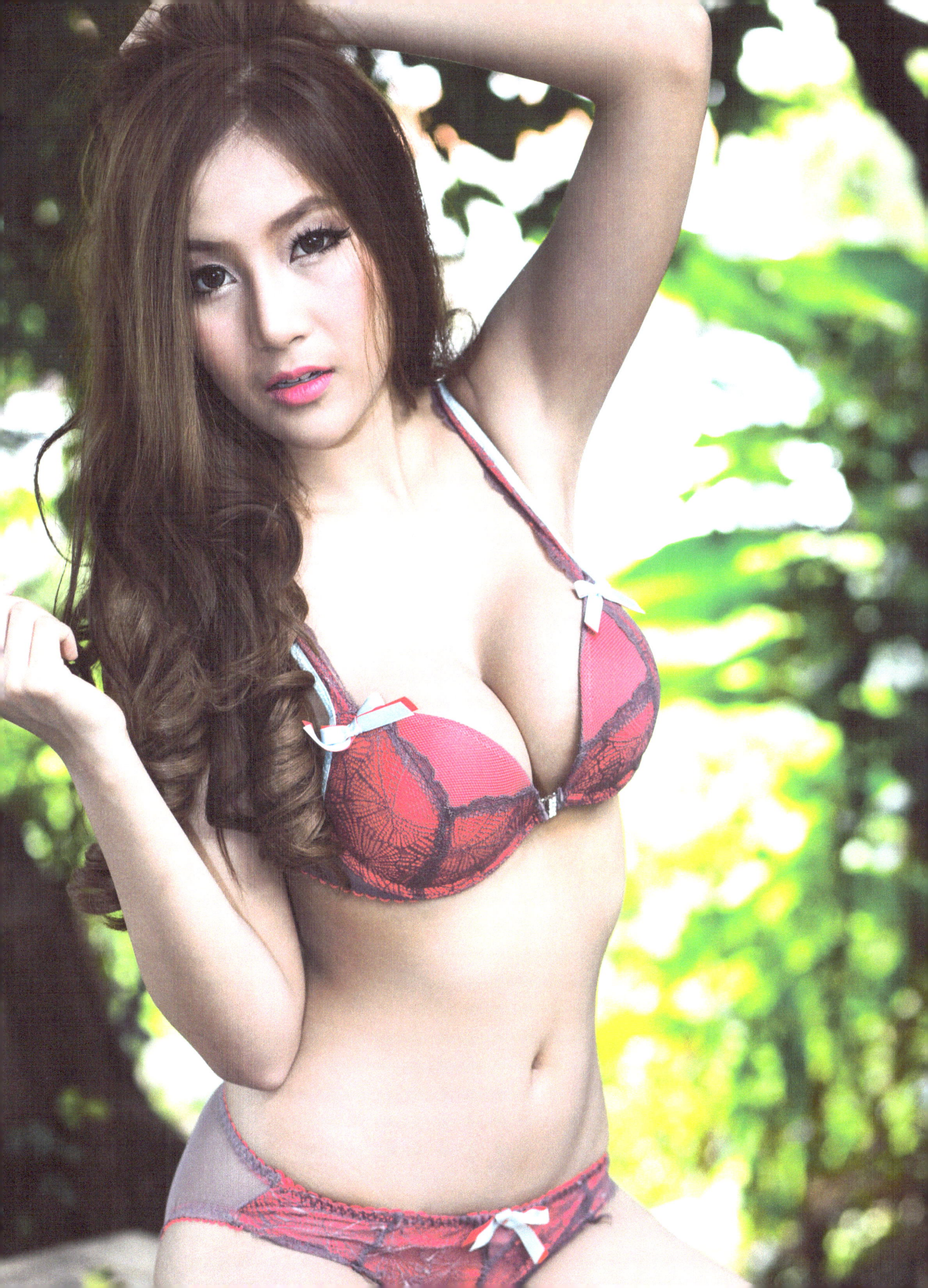

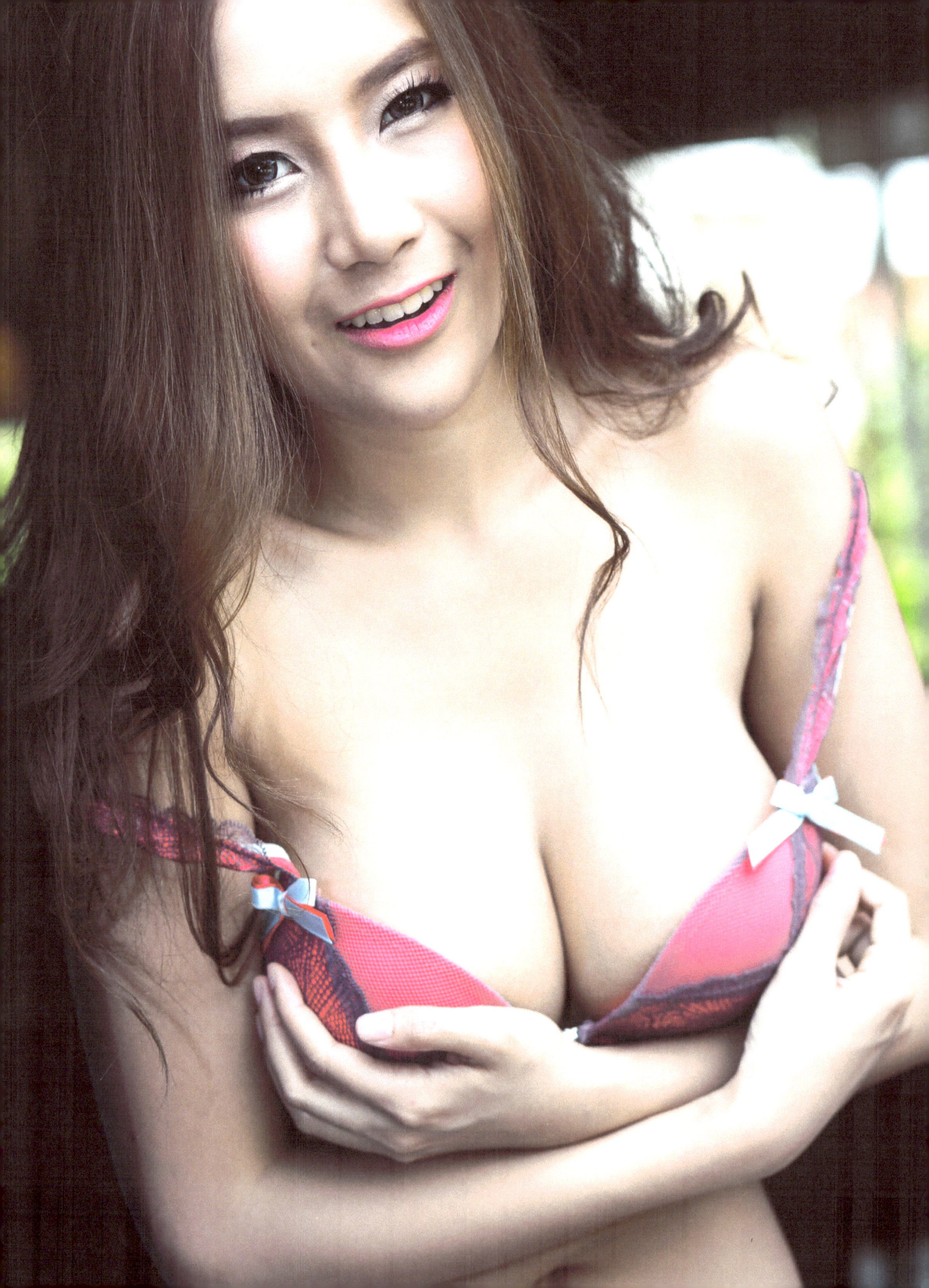

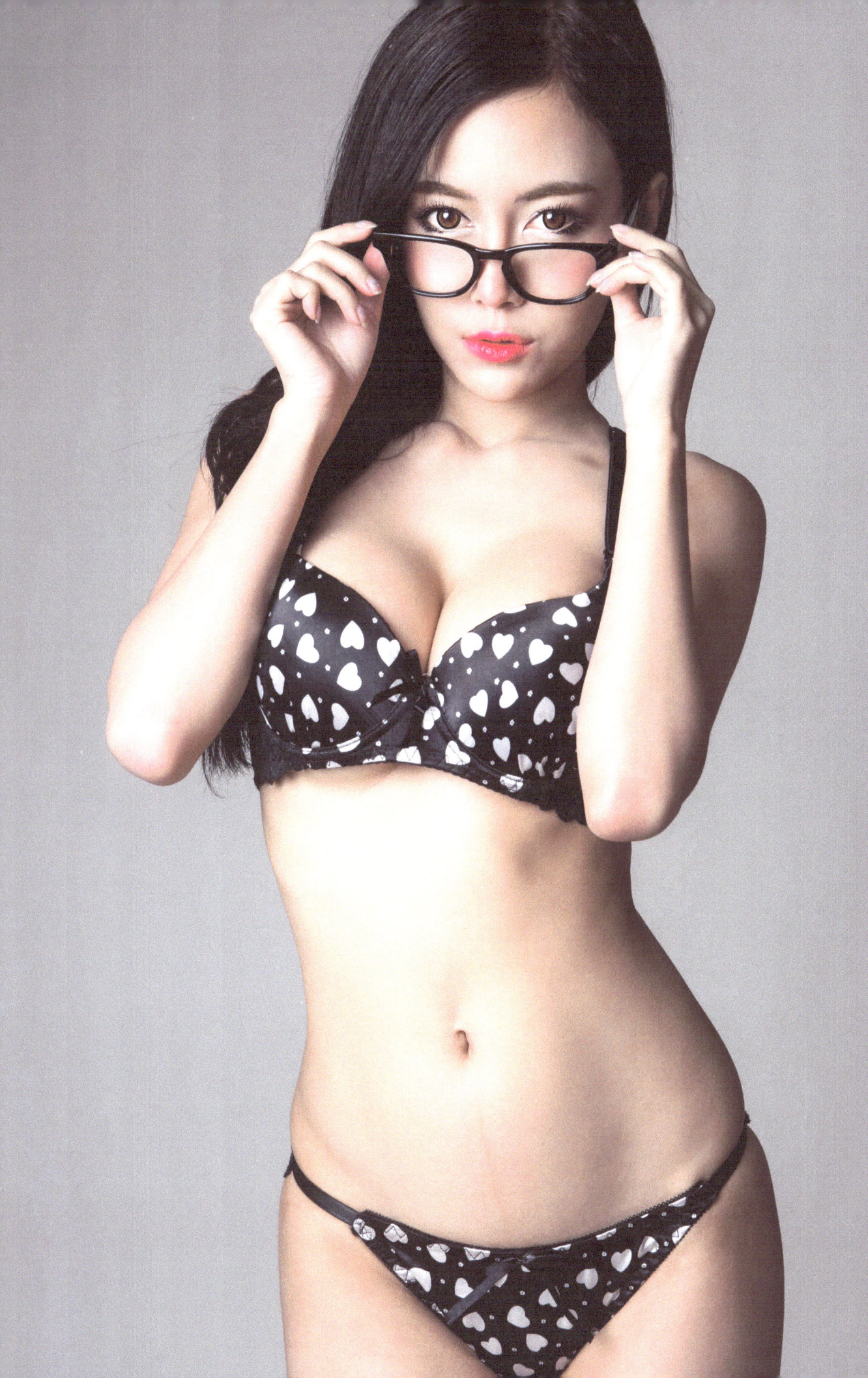

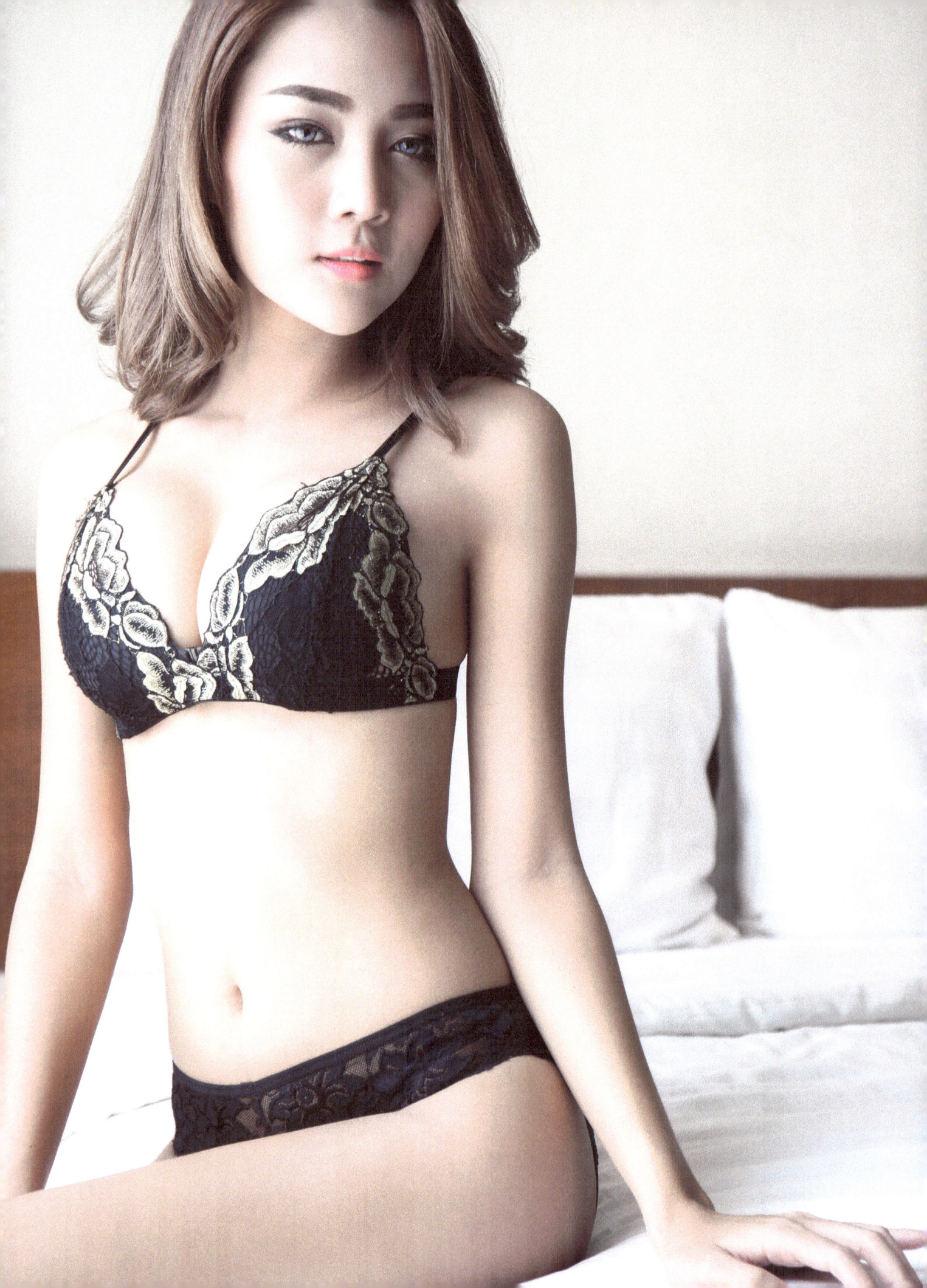

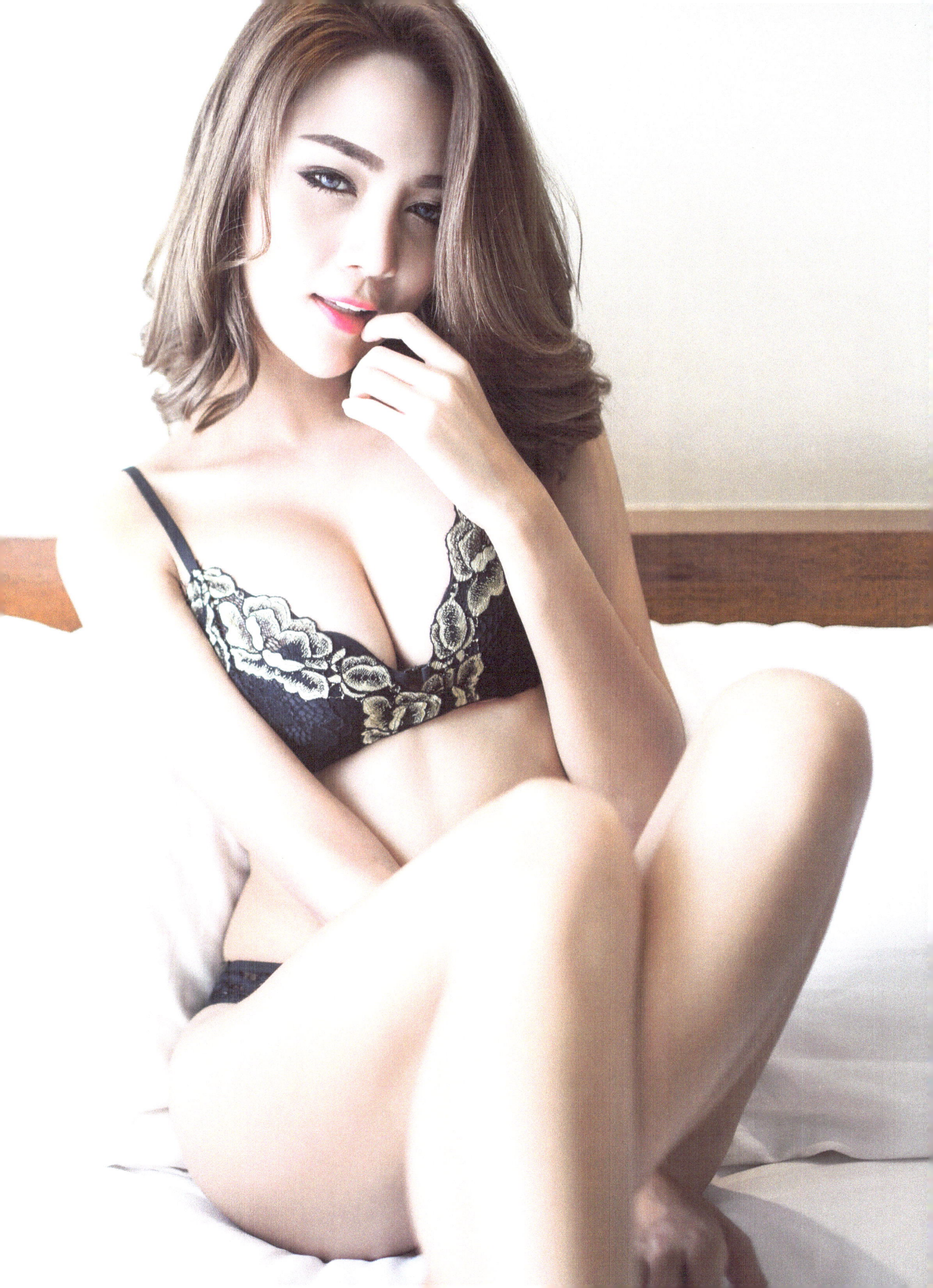

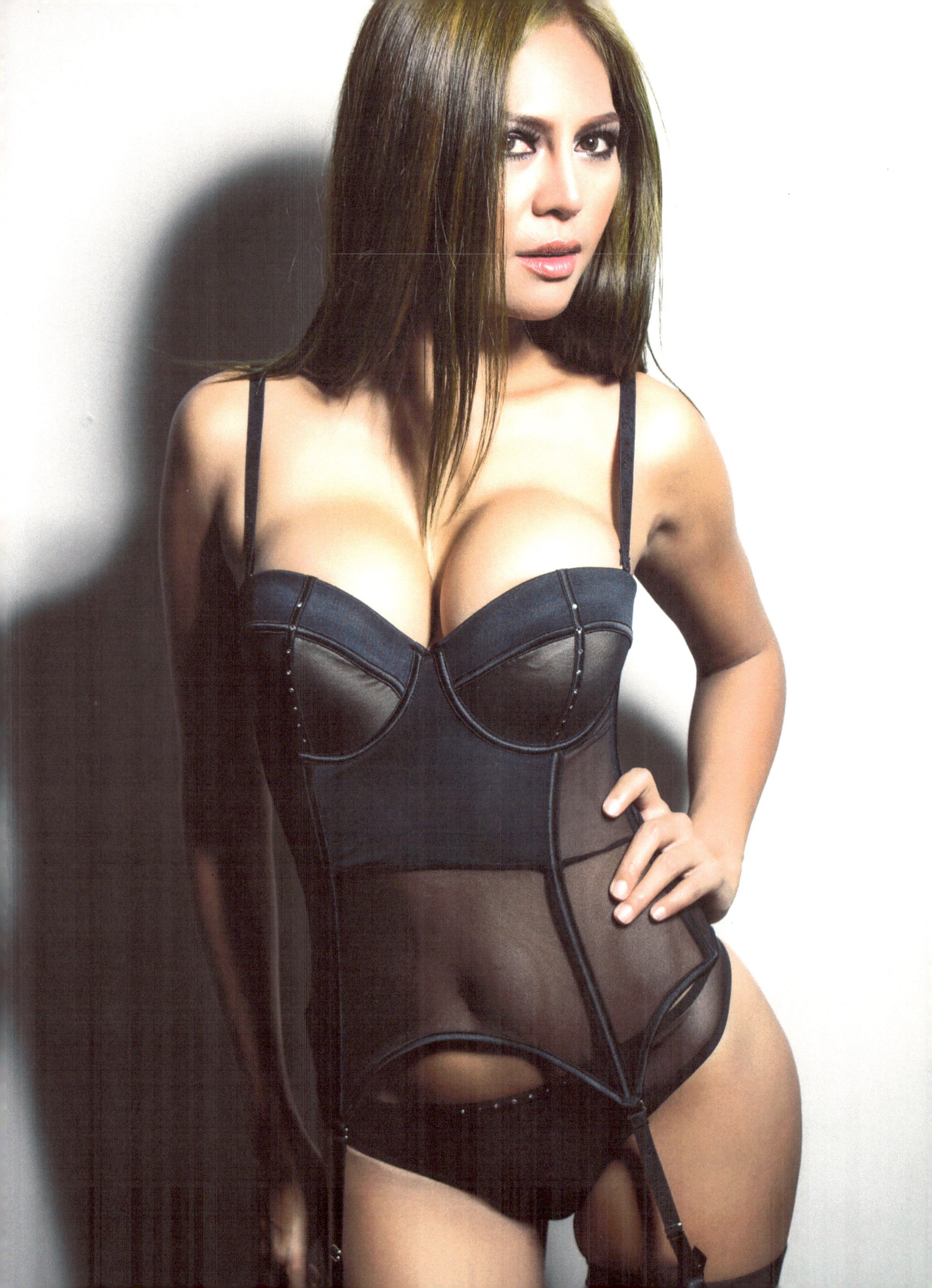

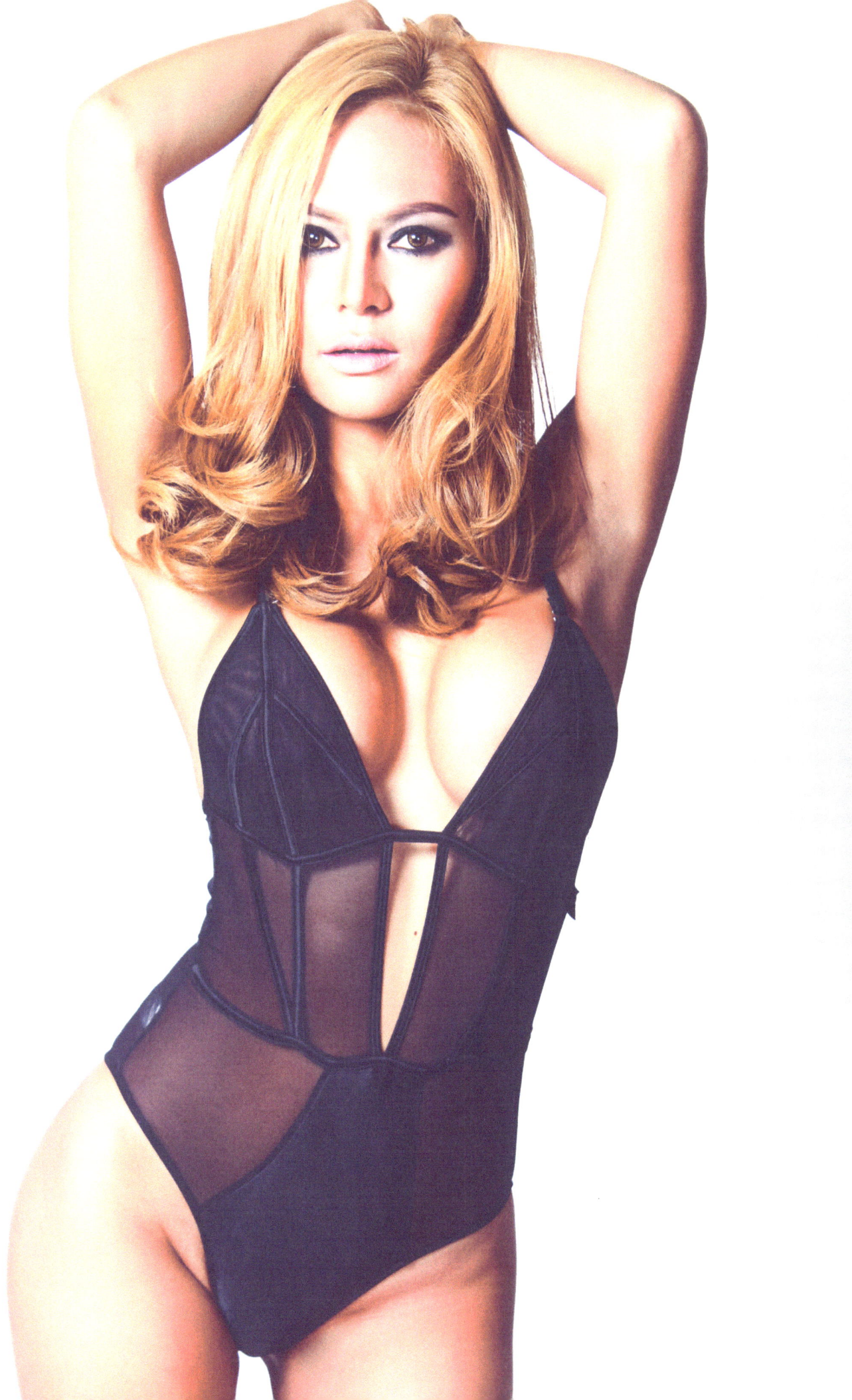

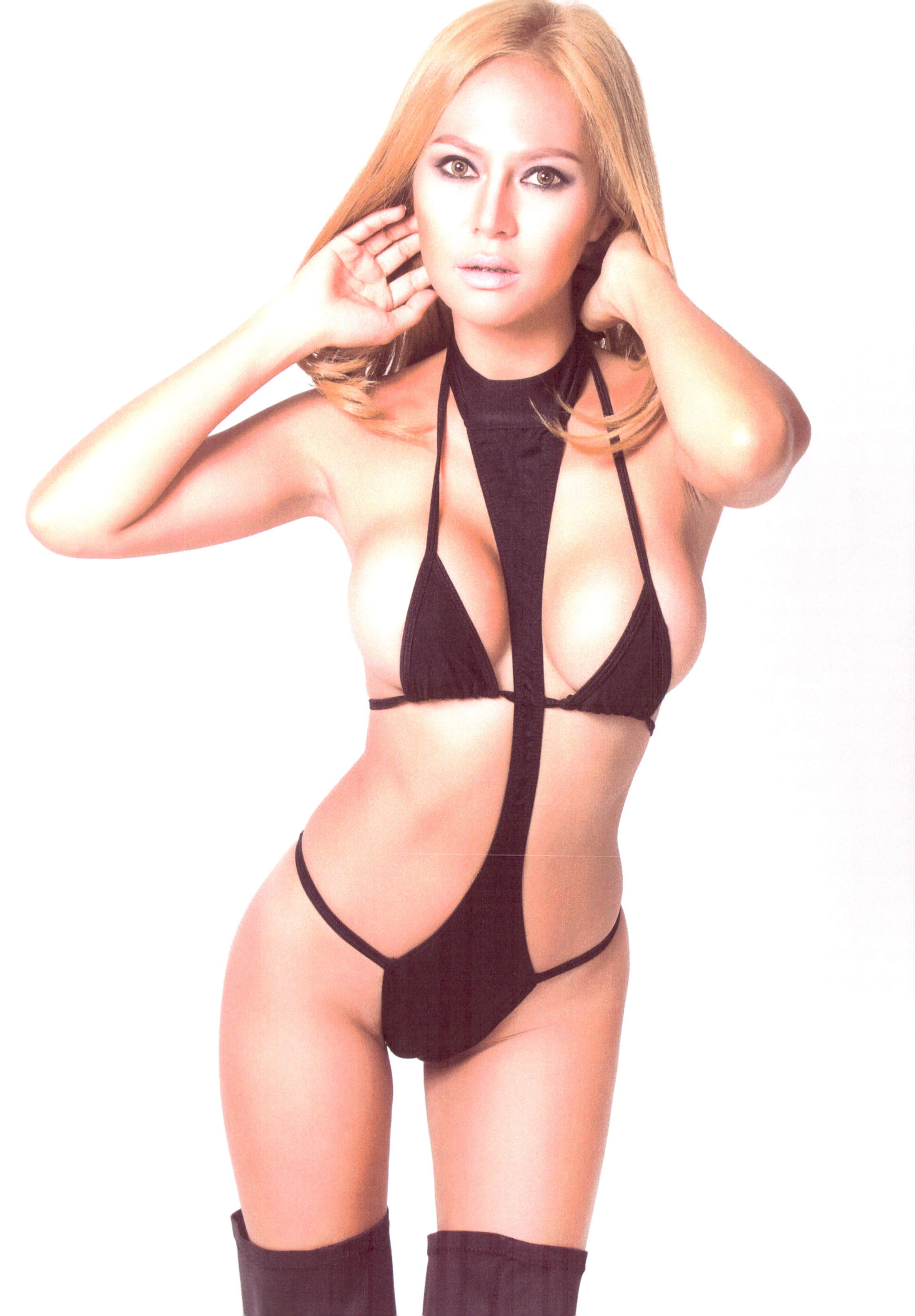

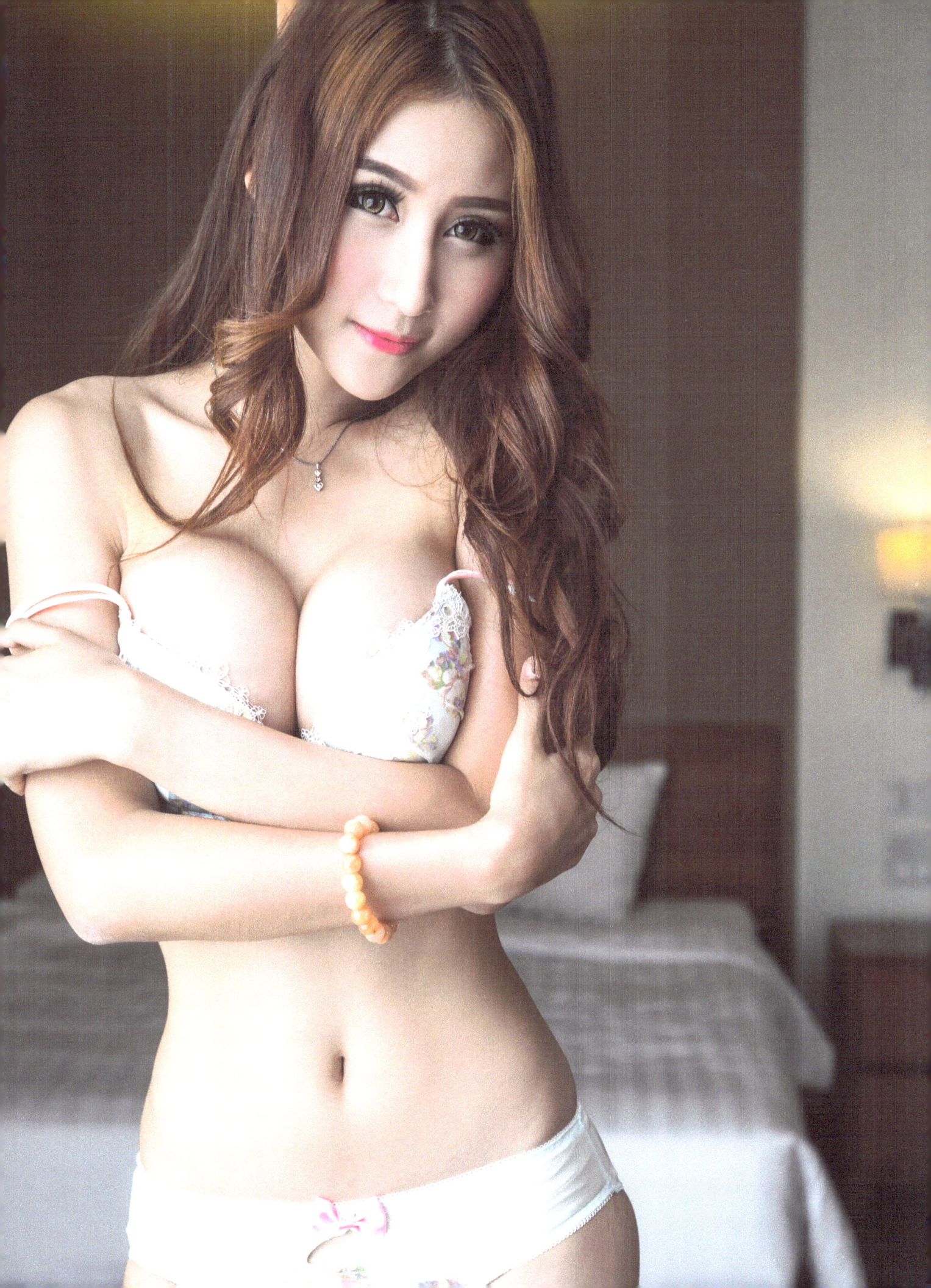

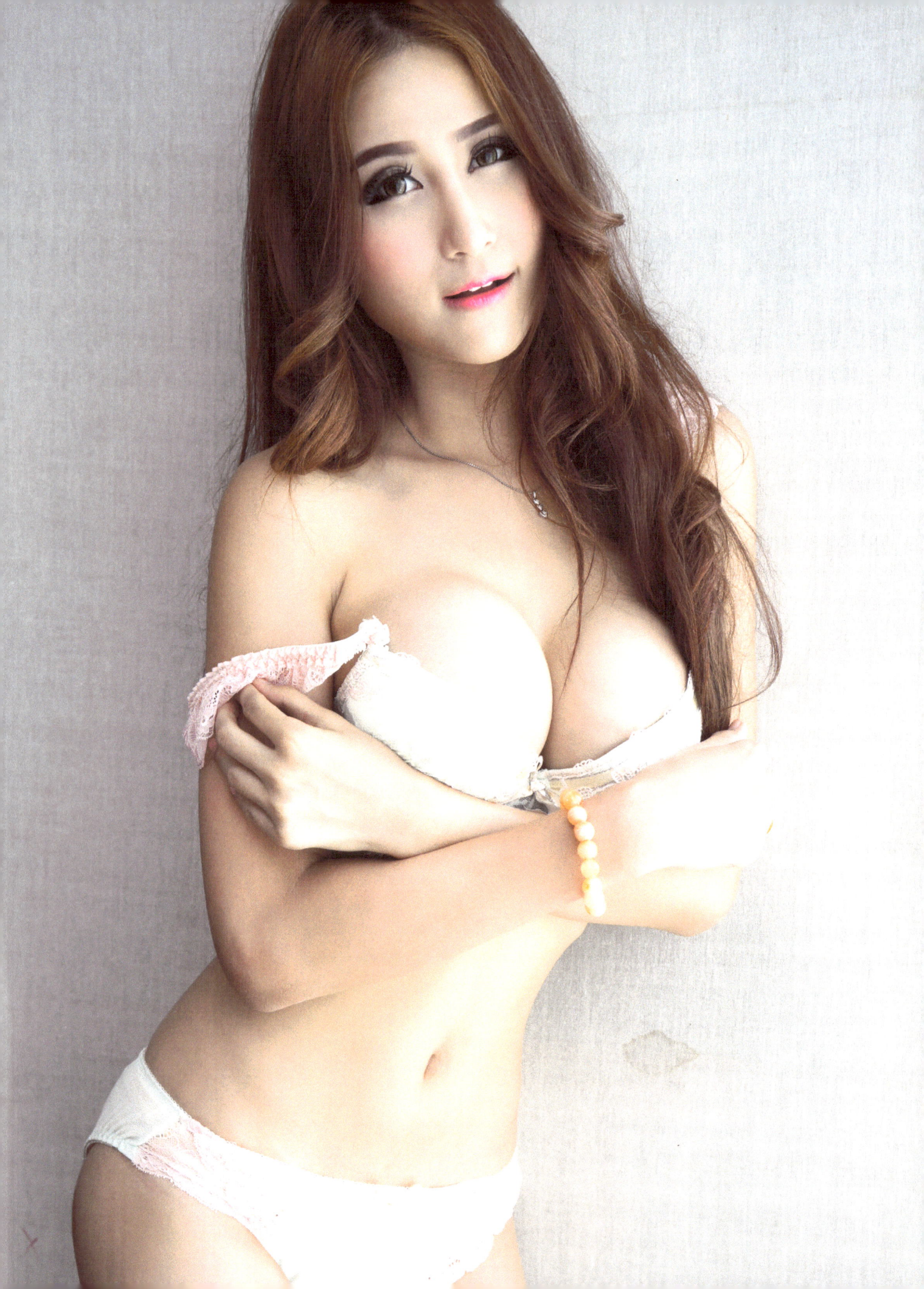

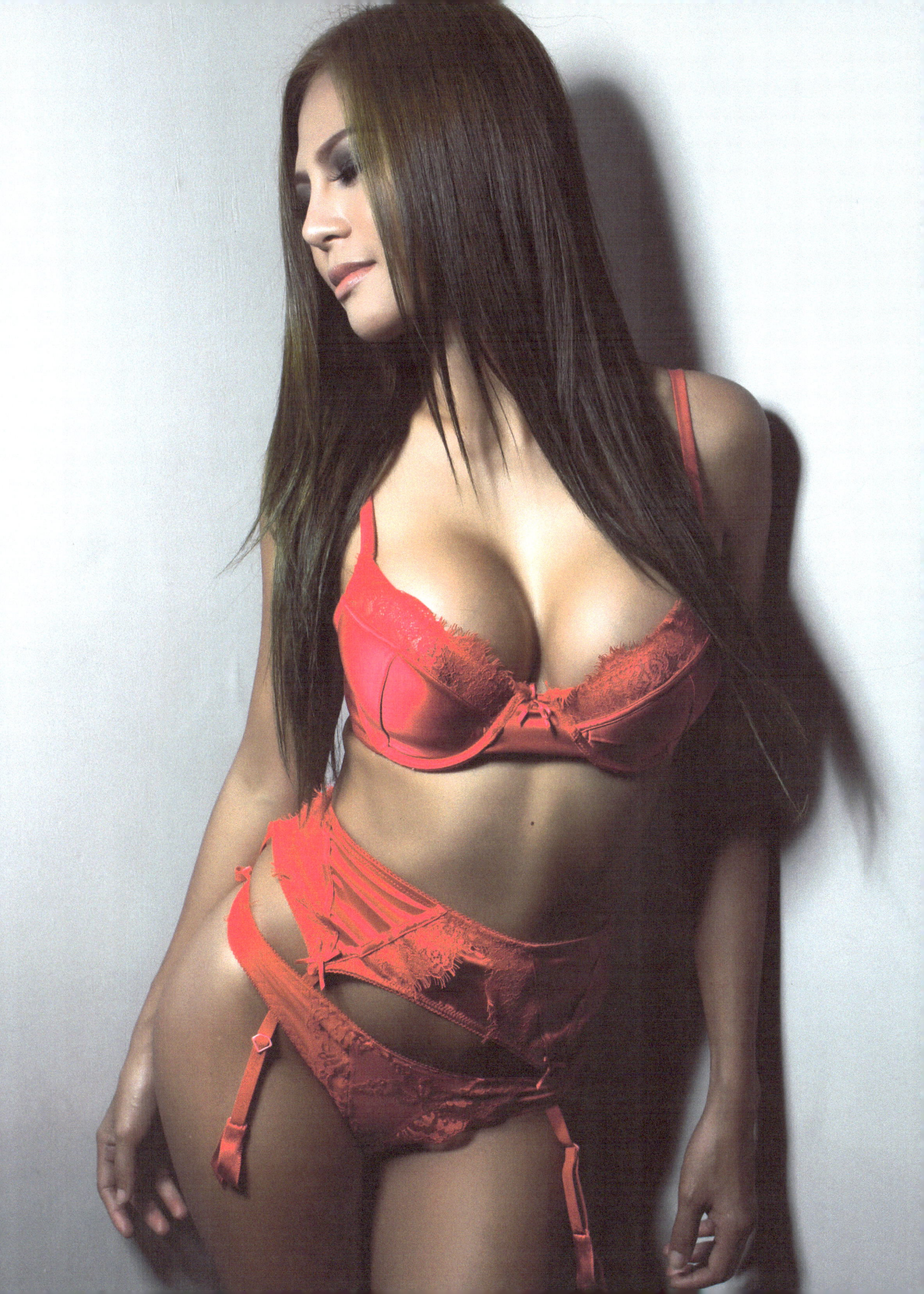

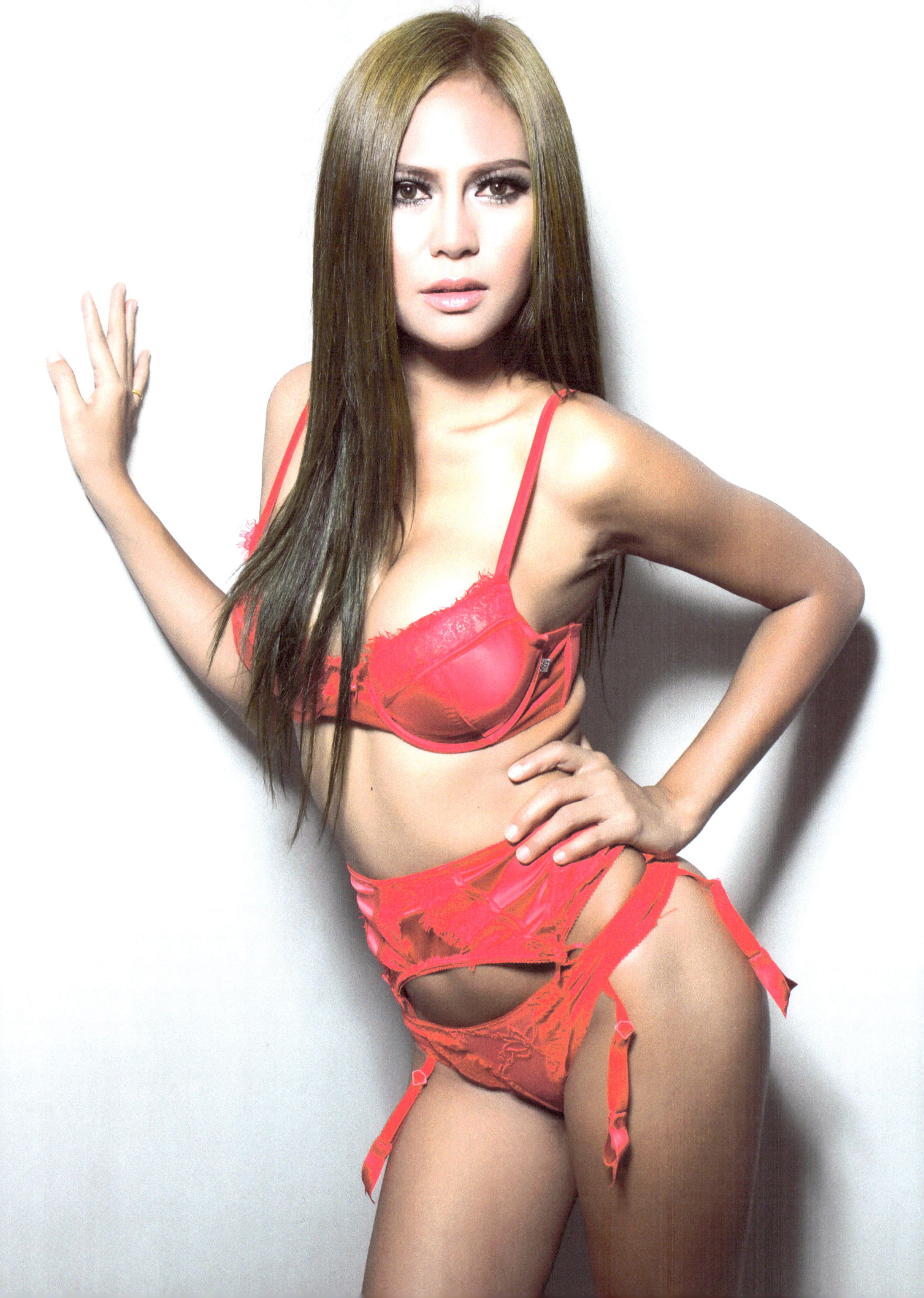

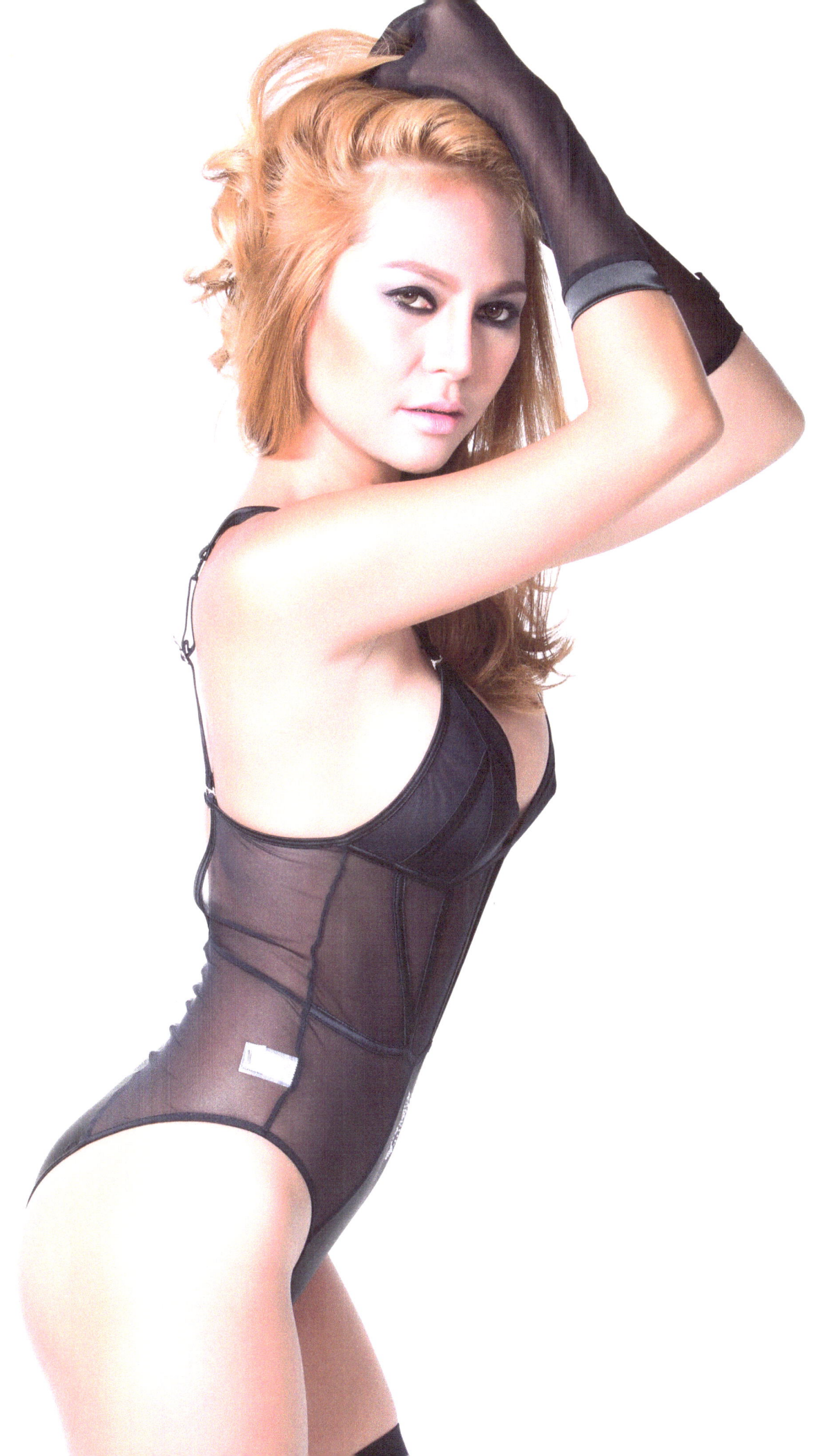

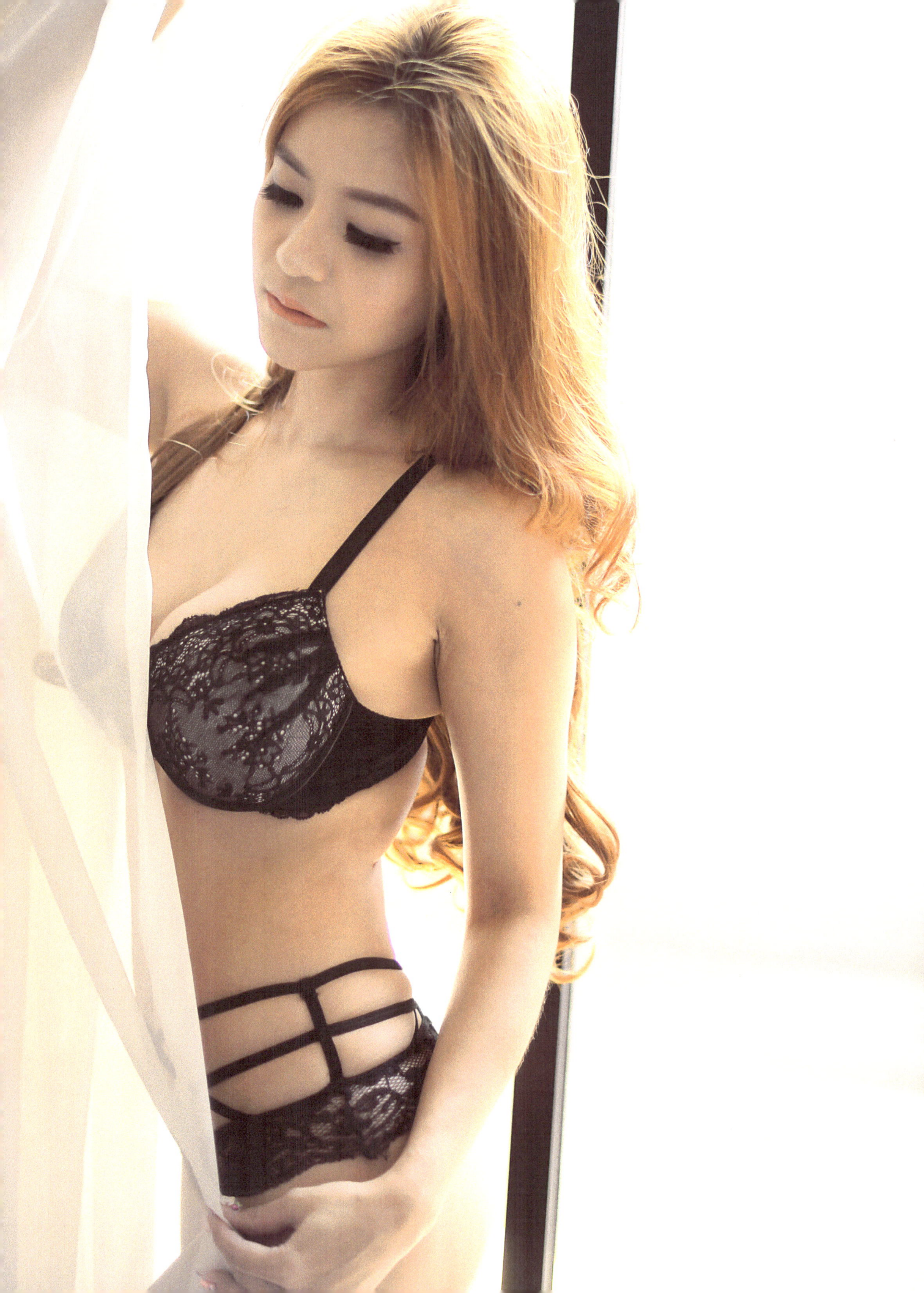

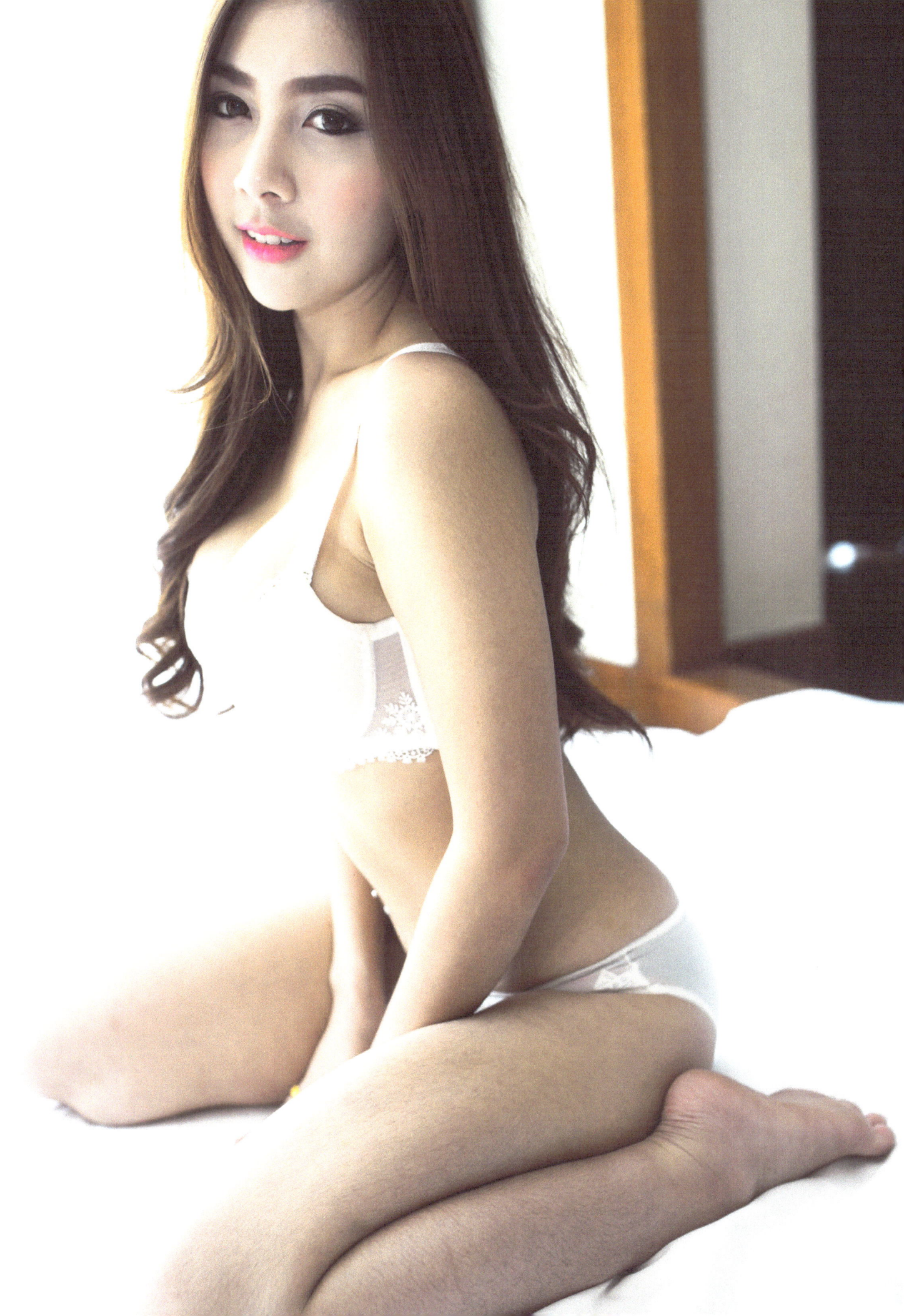

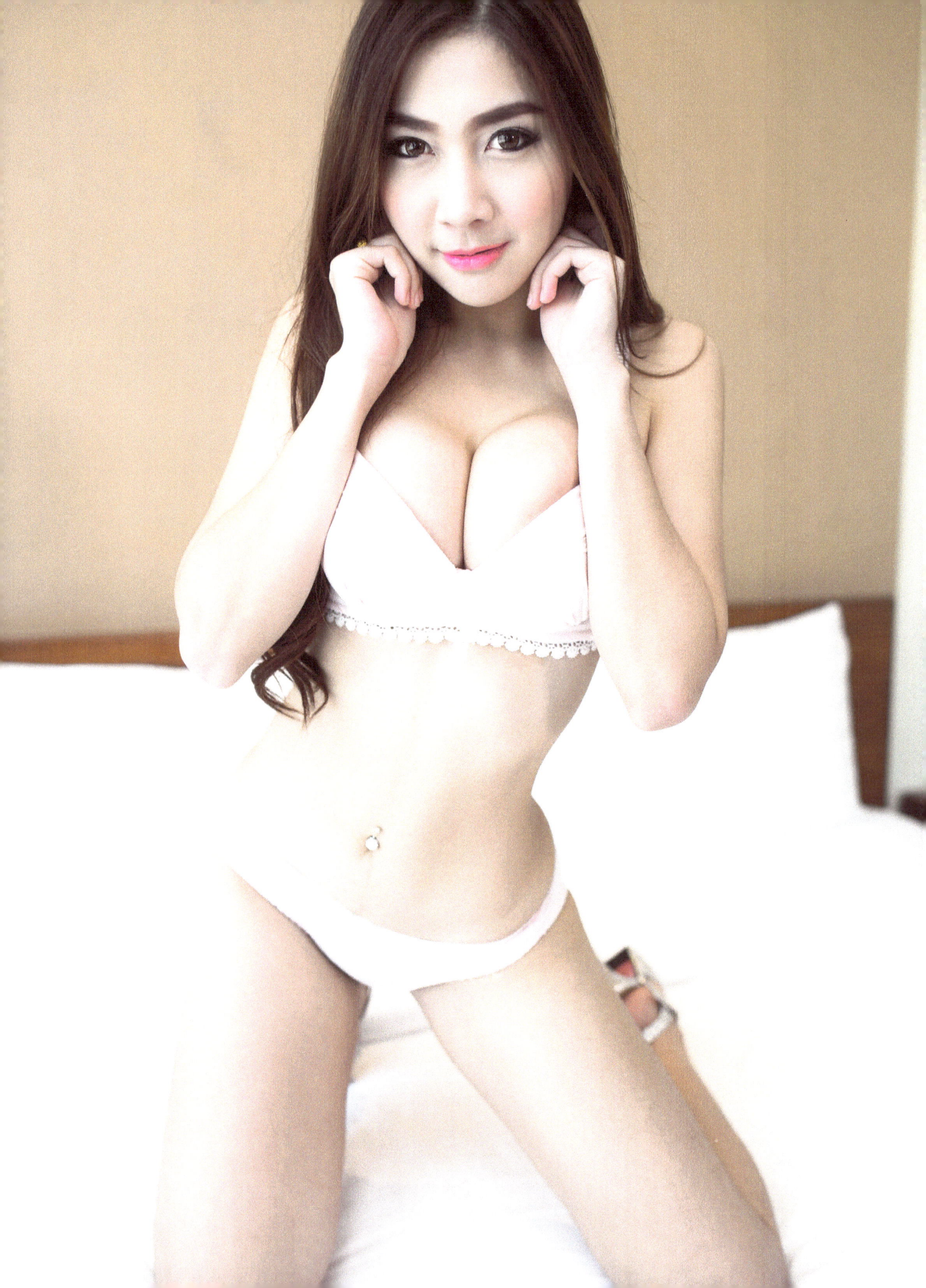

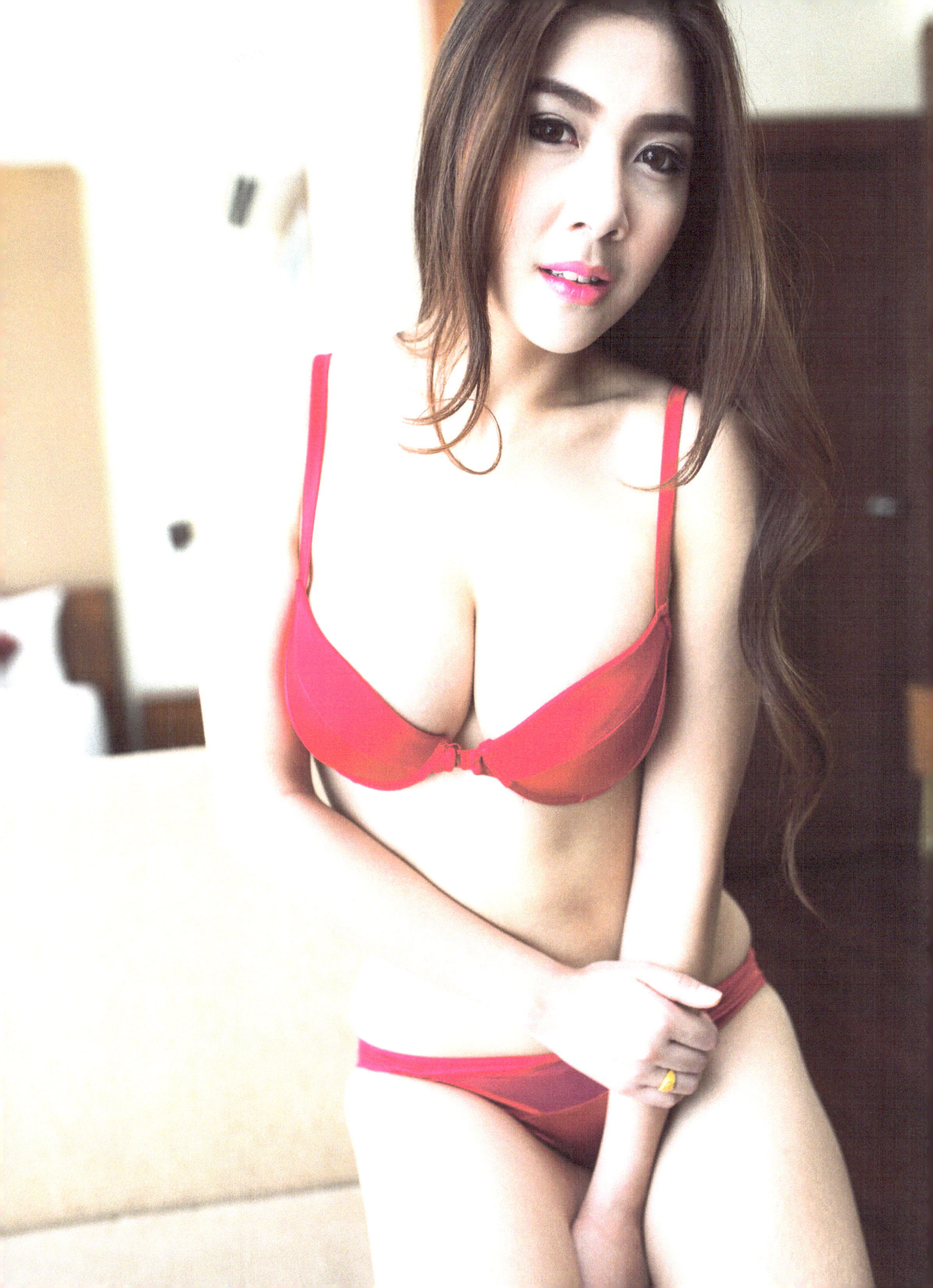

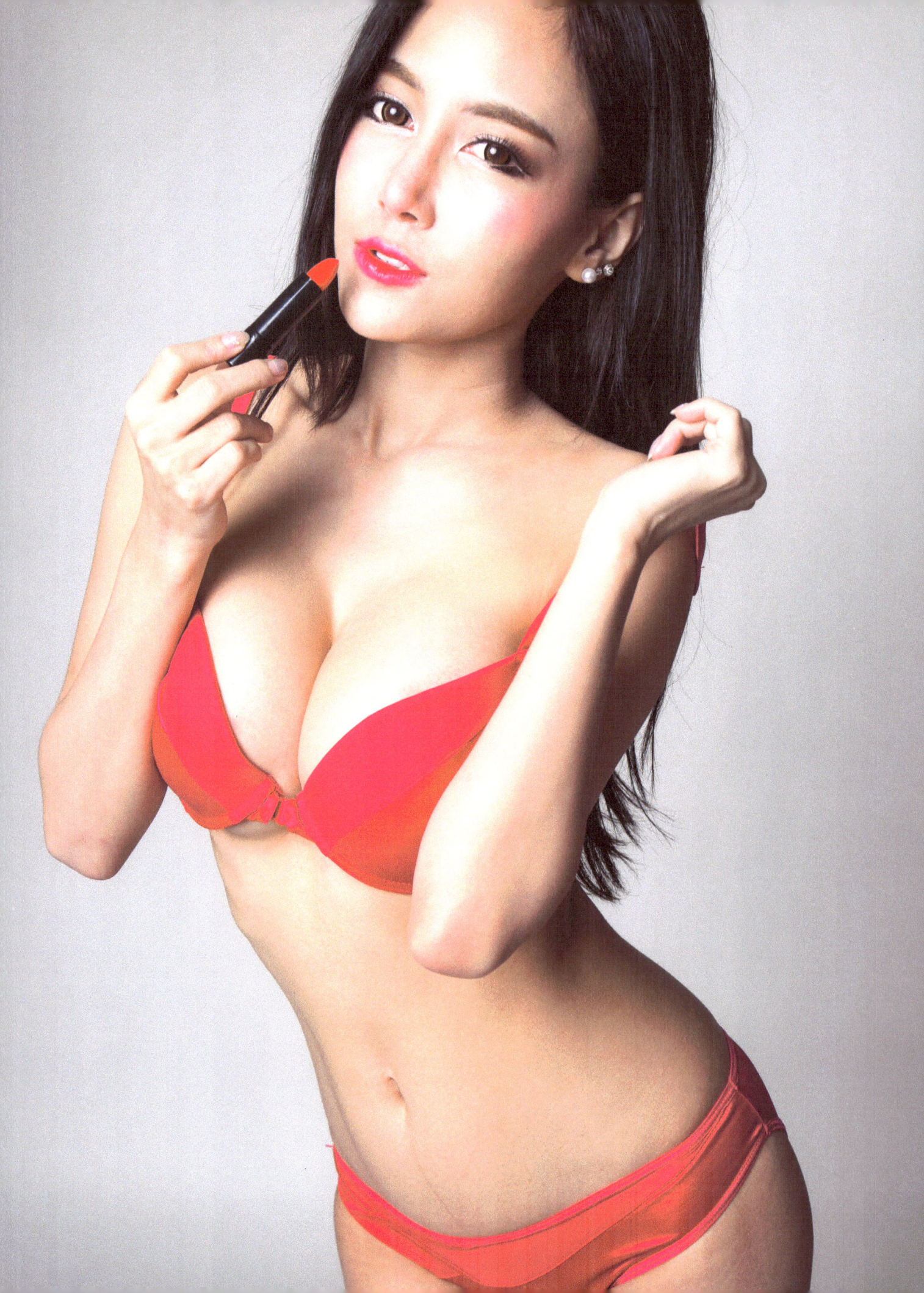

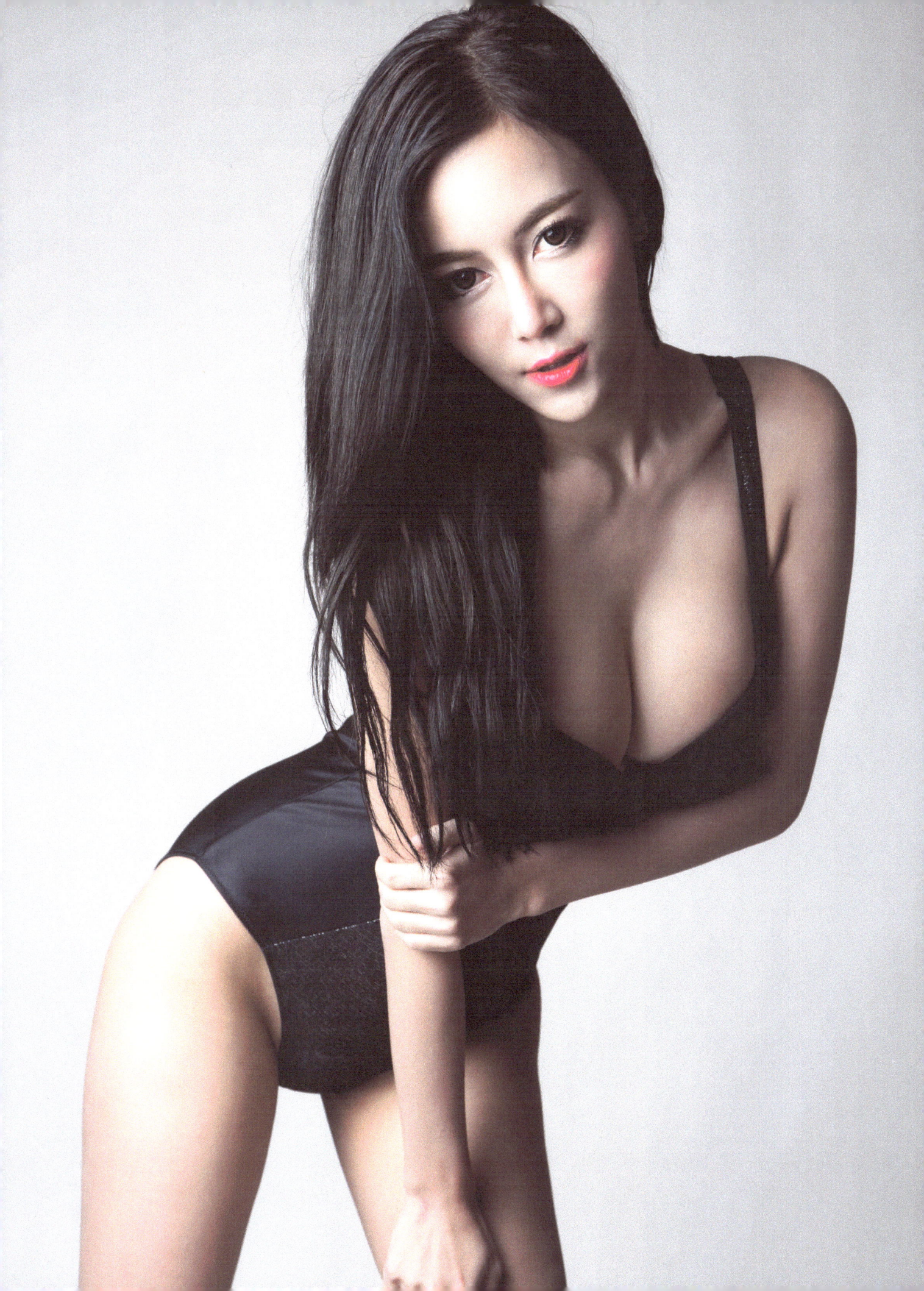

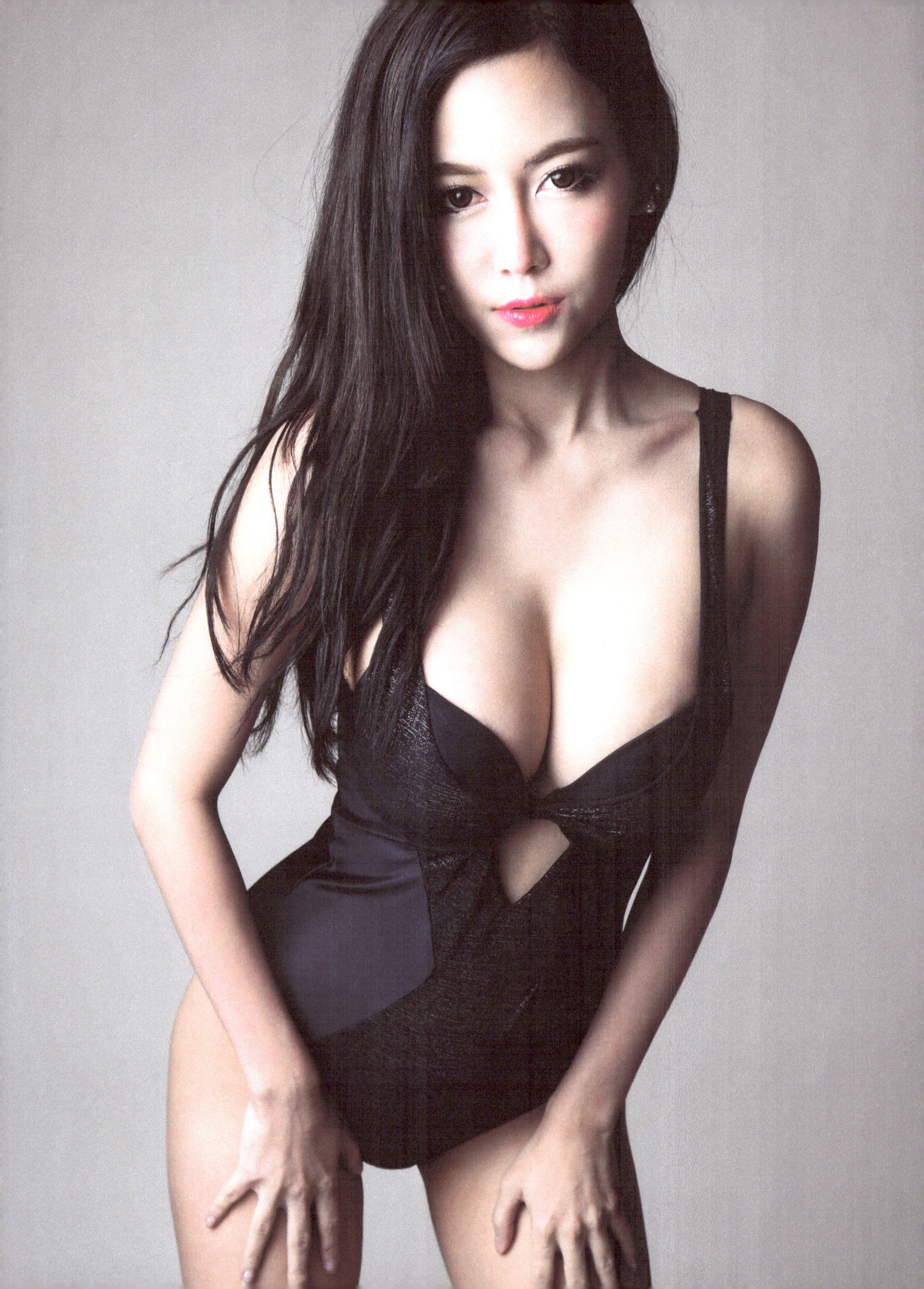

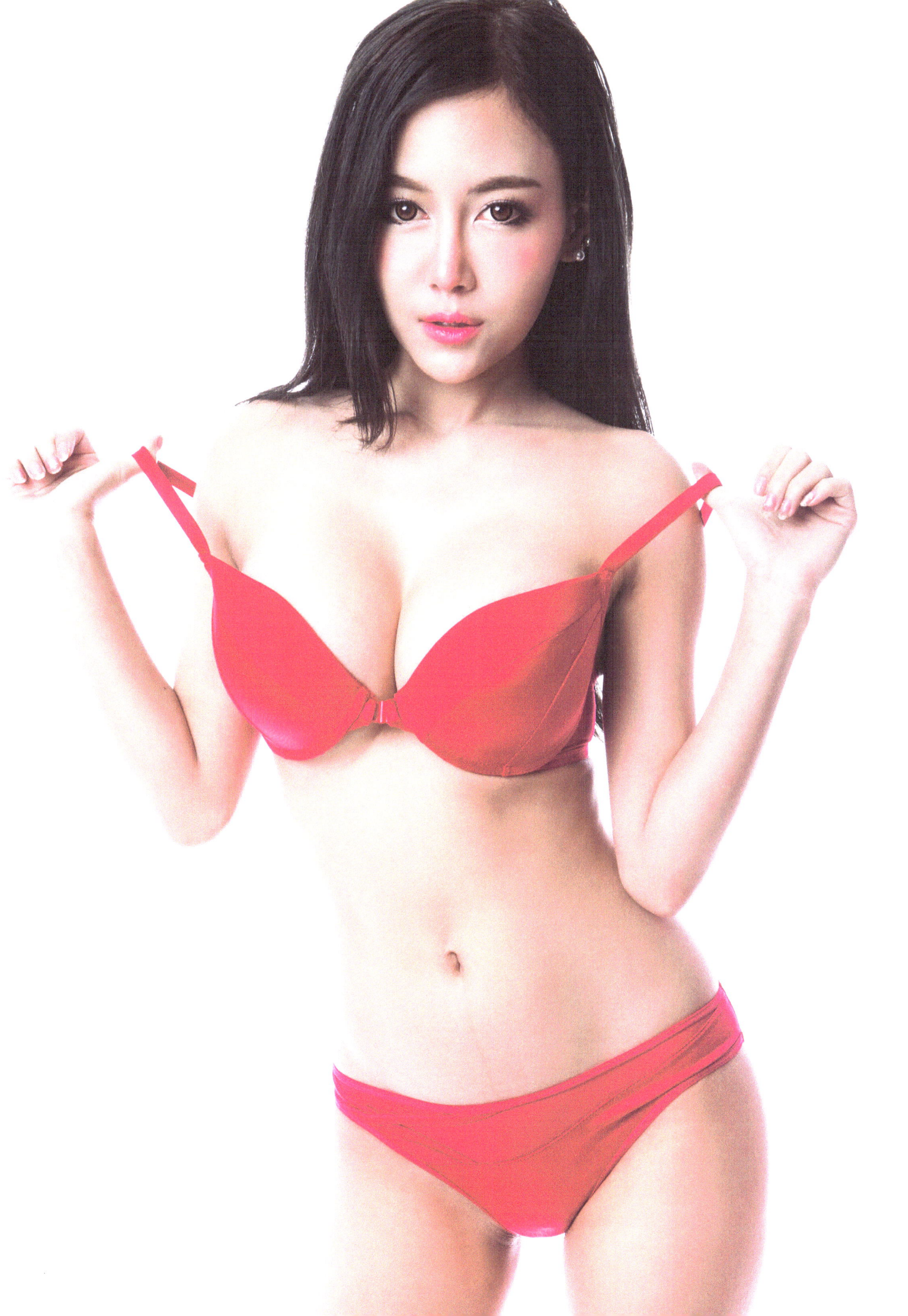

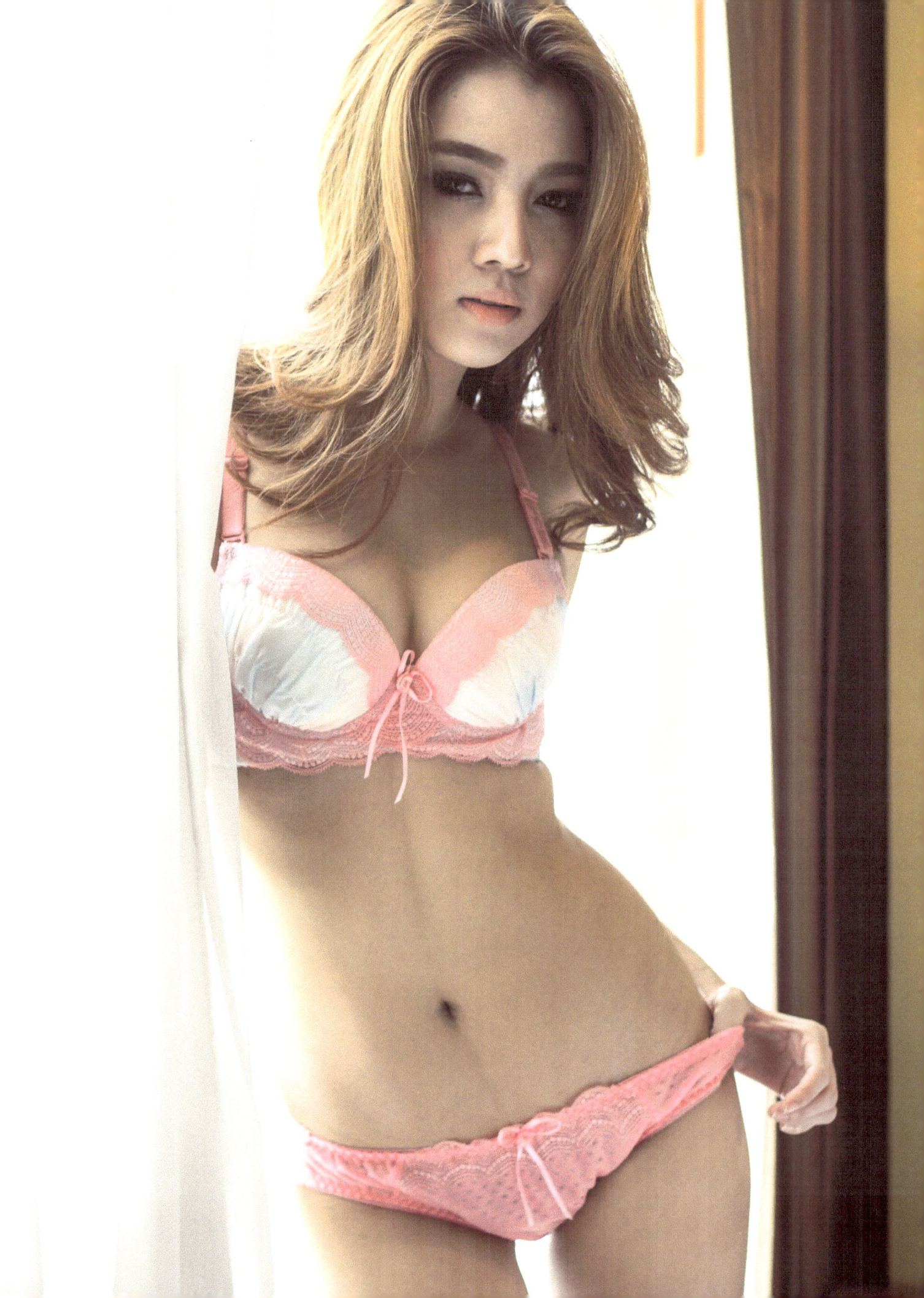

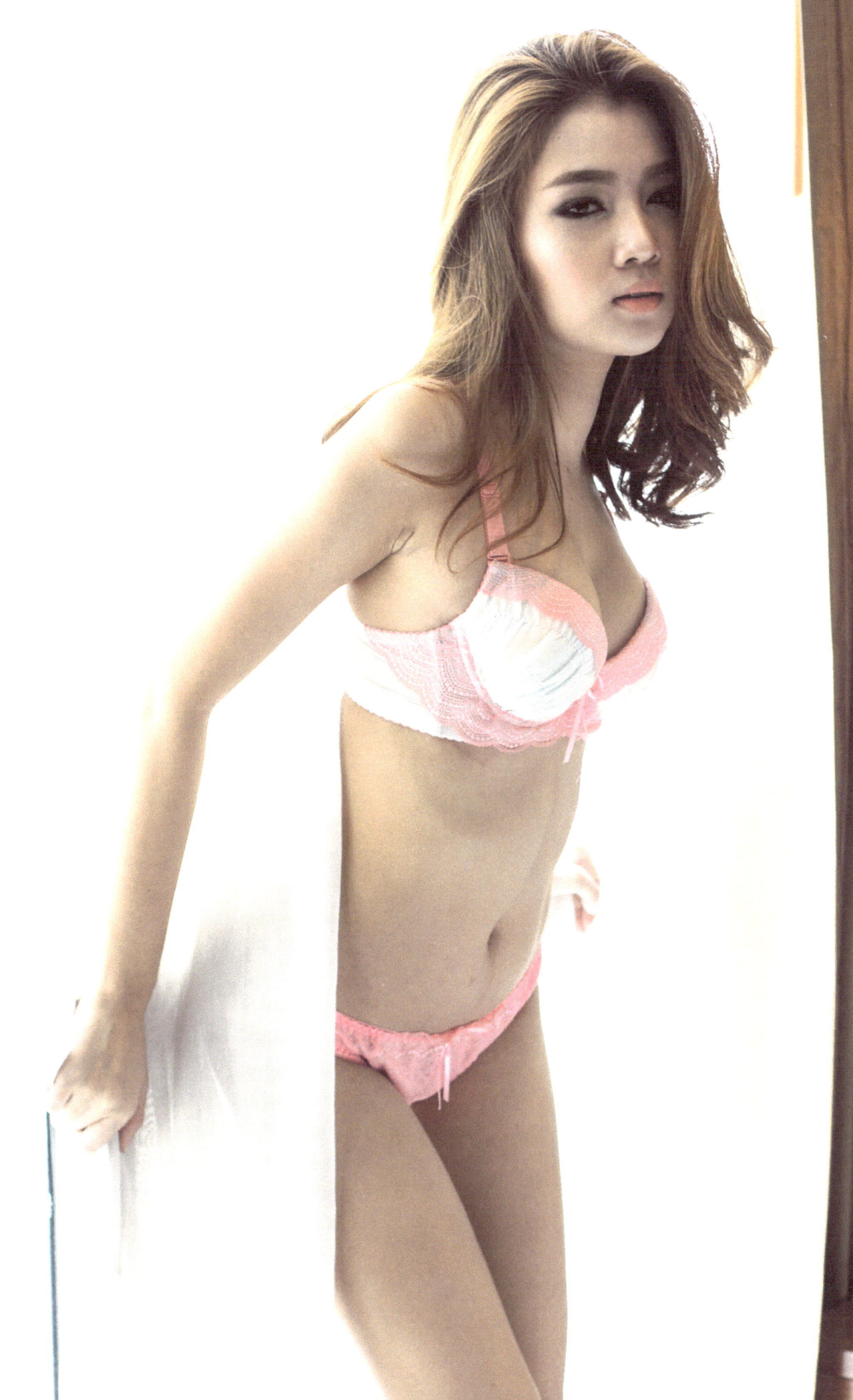

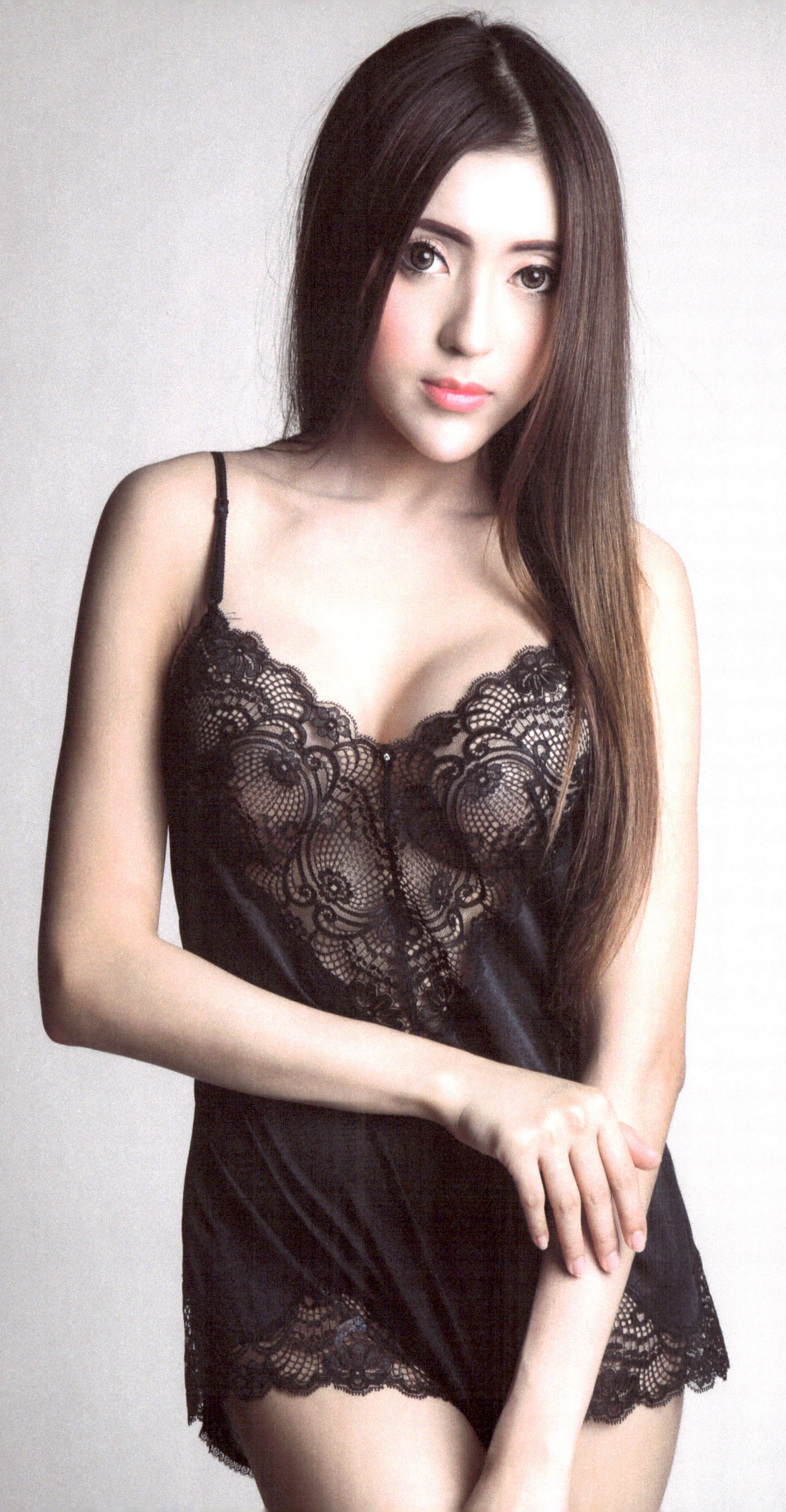

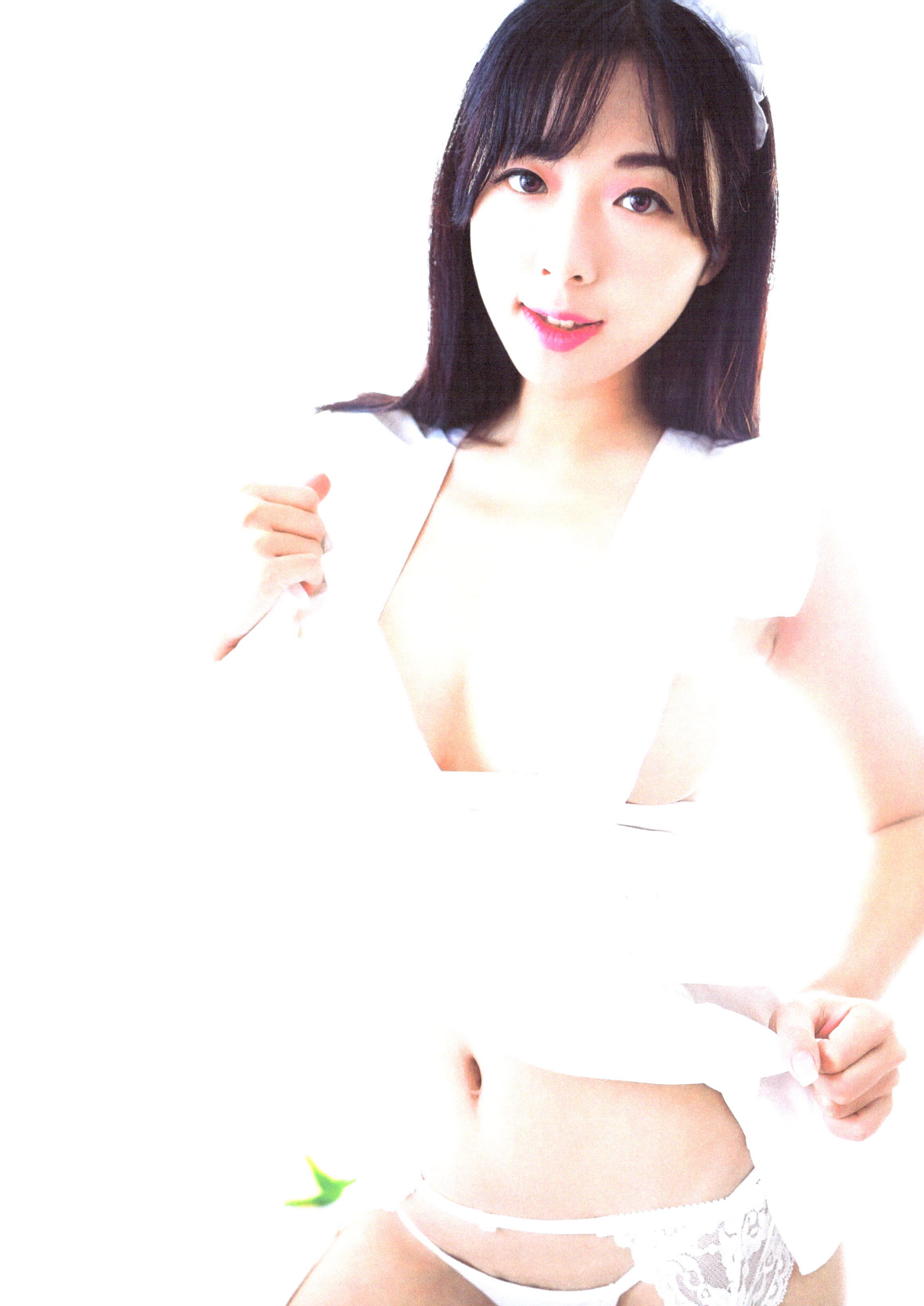

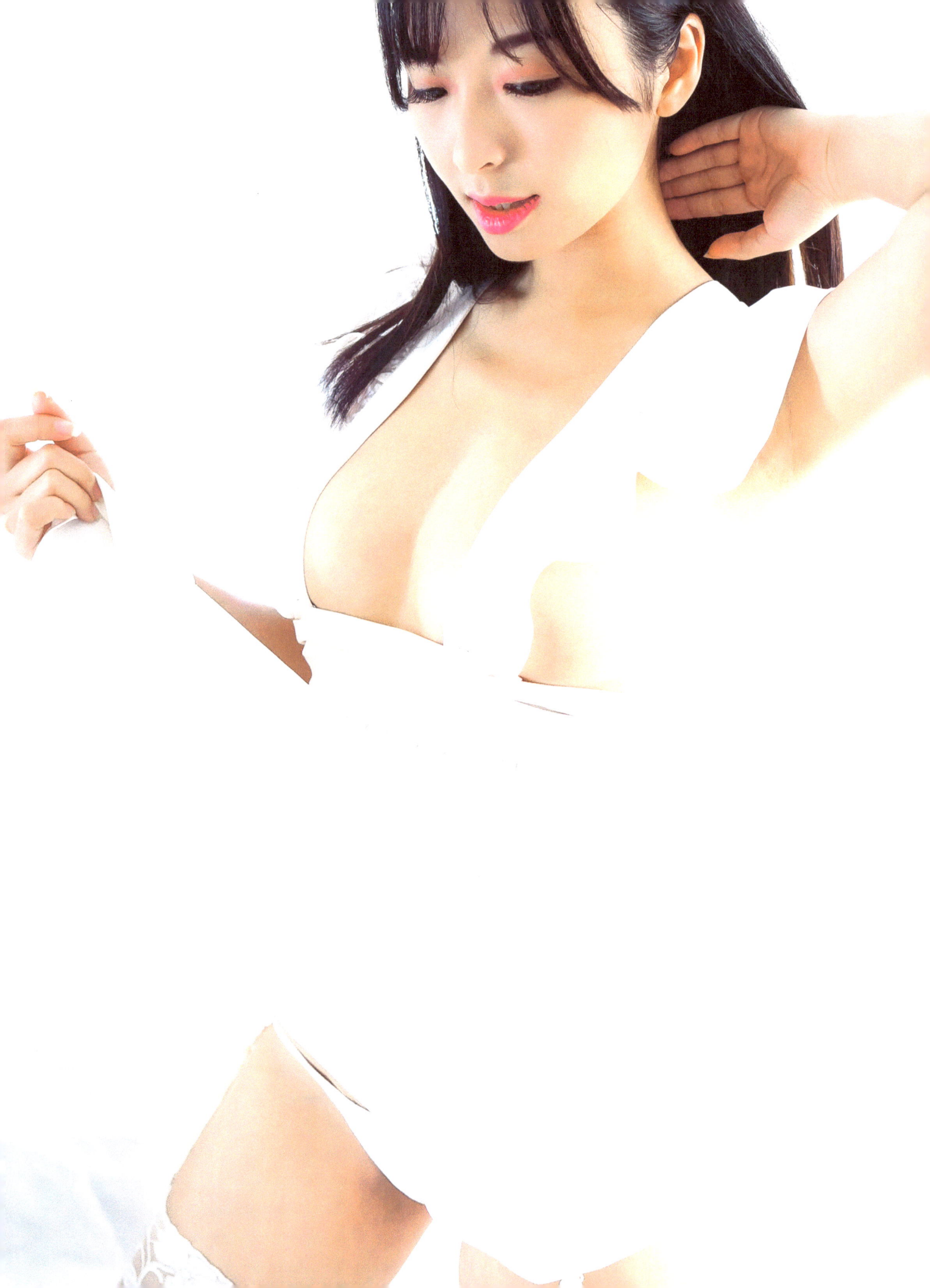

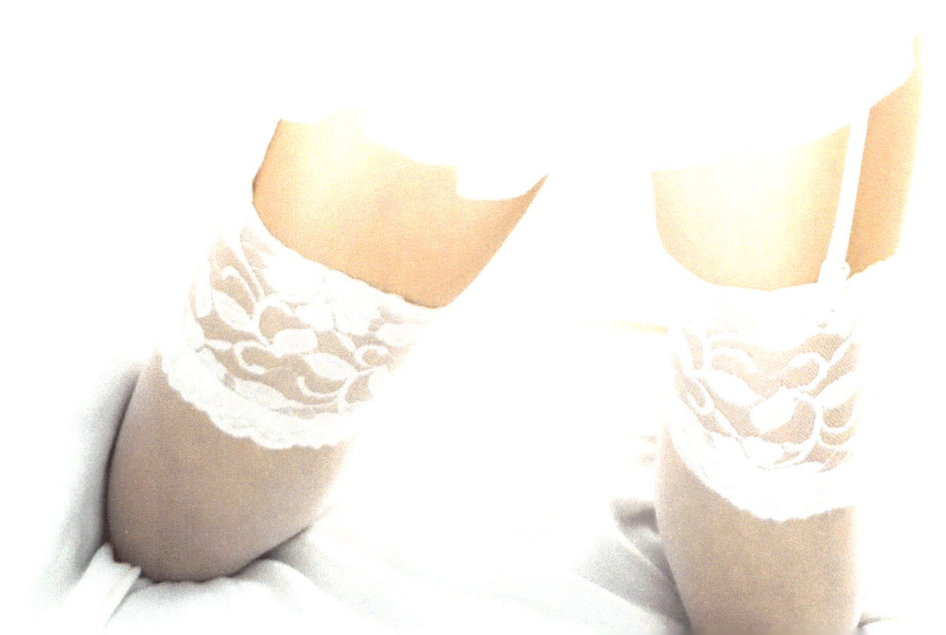

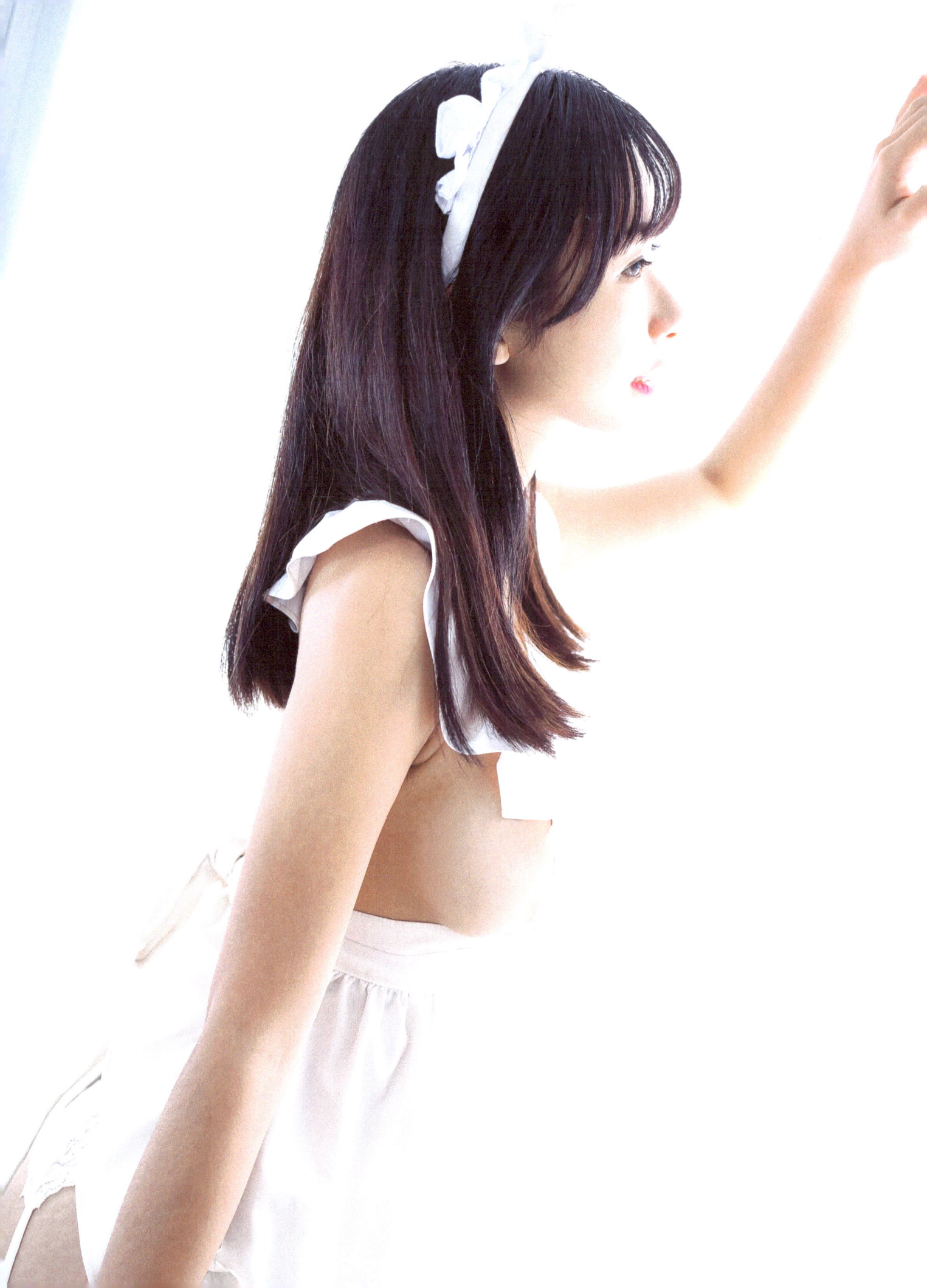

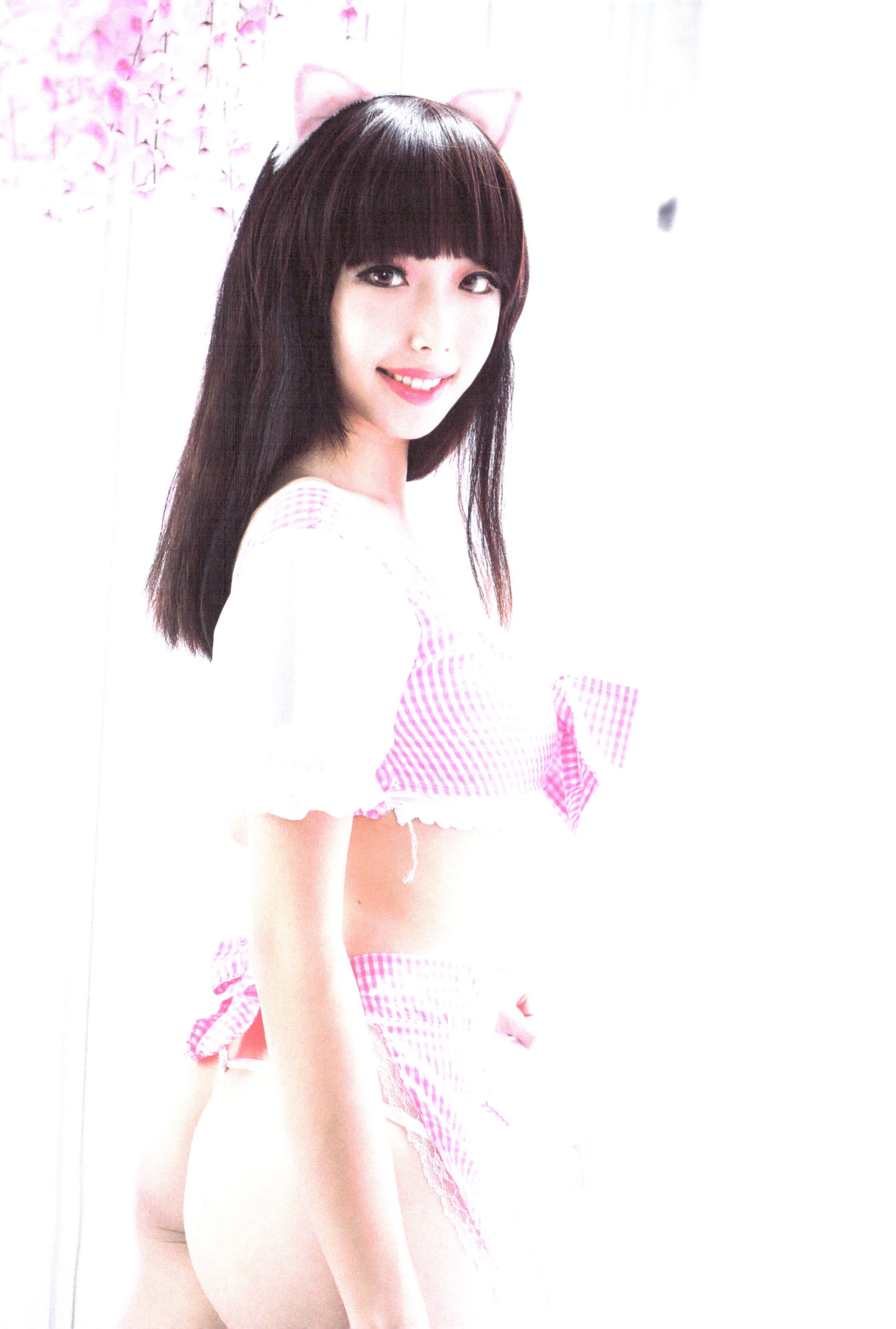

www.ingramcontent.com/pod-product-compliance
Lightning Source LLC
Chambersburg PA
CBHW050420180526

45159CB00005B/2342